**PALM BEACH COUNTY
LIBRARY SYSTEM**
3650 Summit Boulevard
West Palm Beach, FL 33406-4198

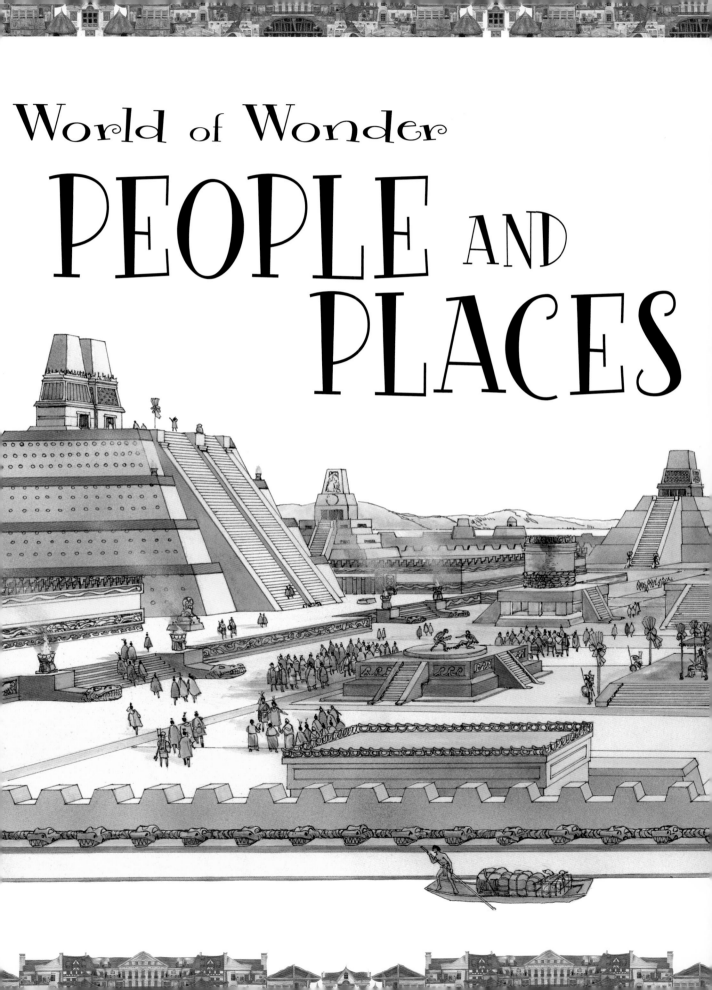

World of Wonder
PEOPLE AND PLACES

Published in Great Britain in 2008 by
The Salariya Book Company Ltd
25 Marlborough Place, Brighton BN1 1UB

ISBN-13: 978-0-531-24028-1 (lib. bdg.)   978-0-531-23824-0 (pbk.)
ISBN-10: 0-531-24028-2 (lib. bdg.)   0-531-23824-5 (pbk.)

A CIP catalog record for this book is available
from the Library of Congress.

Printed and bound in China.

Author: Gerard Cheshire has written many books on
natural history, and over the past twelve years has
cultivated an excellent reputation as an author and
editor. He now lives in Bath, England, with his wife
and three sons.

Artists: David Antram, Mark Bergin, Peter Bull,
C. Constable, Carolyn Franklin, Nicholas Hewetson,
John James, Bob Moulder, Mark Peppé,
Gerald Wood

Editor: Stephen Haynes

Assistant Editor: Rob Walker

Volcano

PAPER FROM
SUSTAINABLE
FORESTS

World of Wonder

People and Places

by Gerard Cheshire

children's press®
An Imprint of Scholastic Inc.
NEW YORK • TORONTO • LONDON • AUCKLAND • SYDNEY
MEXICO CITY • NEW DELHI • HONG KONG
DANBURY, CONNECTICUT

Contents

Where do humans live?

This book is about human beings and the places where they live. Humans have learned to find food, water, and shelter in **climates** across the world. They build shelters to protect them from cold, heat, rain, and wild animals. They can make simple shelters, such as tents and huts, or strong houses of wood, brick, or stone. People can use technology to survive even in space.

Where Did the First People Live?

The earliest humans lived on the continent of Africa. Many scientists believe that the East African Rift Valley is where the first people lived.

Many animals have horns, claws, or sharp teeth to protect themselves and fur to keep them warm. Early humans had none of these things. They had to use their brains to invent tools, weapons, shelters, clothing, and ways of making fire. Once they had these things, they spread out from Africa to almost every part of the world.

Europe

Africa

Elephant

East African
Rift Valley

Bison

Mammoth

Musk ox

Bear

Asia

Deer

Horse

Tiger

True or False?

Fire was first used
8,000 years ago.

?
?
?

Answers on page 31

Australia

The arrows on the map show
how humans spread from
Africa to the rest of the world.

Who Were the First Artists?

People have made pictures and sculptures for thousands of years. The oldest surviving pictures were painted or scratched on the walls of caves. They include very realistic drawings of animals.

It must have been hard work to make these pictures—many of them are in places that are dark and difficult to reach. Perhaps the artists believed that the pictures would bring them success in their hunting.

Who Were the First Farmers?

The first people were **hunter-gatherers**. They moved around, hunting animals and picking fruits and other parts of plants for food. They lived in shelters that could be moved easily. Later, some groups learned to grow crops and keep farm animals. They were able to build villages and live in one place all the time.

Movable shelters

True or False?

Early hunter-gatherers used the bones of mammoths to build their huts.

Answers on page 31

Domesticated oxen, horses, and donkeys could also be used for pulling and carrying heavy loads.

An important part of farming was the **domestication** of cattle. Cows provided meat, milk, leather, and other valuable materials.

Why farm the land?

Domesticated crops produced far more food than wild plants. More people could be fed, and villages could become larger.

The Sumerian people of Mesopotamia (the area that is now called Iraq) had large-scale farming more than 7,000 years ago.

Ancient Sumerian farmers

Where Were the First Cities?

The oldest cities that we know about were in a part of the Middle East known as the Fertile Crescent. It had rich soil and plenty of water and sunshine—perfect for farming.

Indus Valley

Çatal Hüyük

Sumer

Fertile Crescent

Çatal Hüyük

Sumer

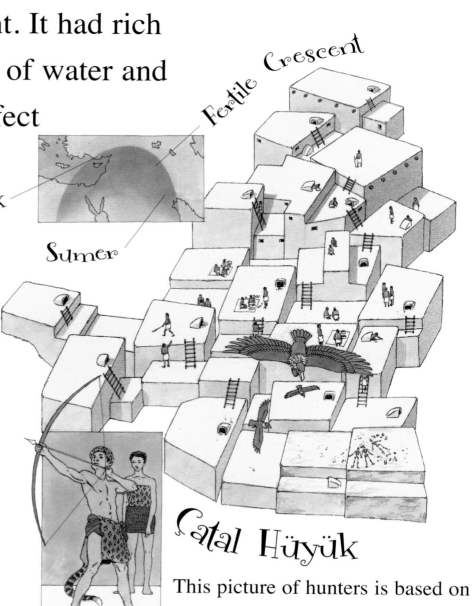

Çatal Hüyük was a city in the Fertile Crescent, in what is now Turkey. It was built about 9,500 years ago. The mud-brick houses were entered through holes in the roof.

Çatal Hüyük

This picture of hunters is based on a wall painting at Çatal Hüyük.

Sumer

Crops grew easily in the Fertile Crescent, so farmers often had more food than they needed for themselves. Farmers came to the cities to sell their spare food and buy things that they could not make themselves. The Sumerian cities of ancient Iraq grew large and busy.

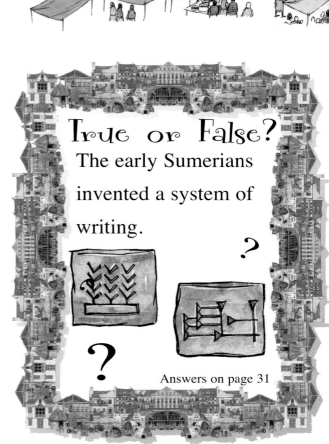

Mohenjo-Daro

Other important early cities were built in the Indus Valley, in present-day India and Pakistan, about 5,000 years ago. The most famous ancient cities in the Indus Valley are Harappa and Mohenjo-Daro.

True or False?

The early Sumerians invented a system of writing.

?

?

?

Answers on page 31

What Is the Most Populated Place?

China

The most populated country in the world is China. One fifth of the world's population lives in China—more than 1.3 billion people. The Chinese people are encouraged to have just one child per family so that the population will not grow so quickly.

Rice is a crop with a long stalk which gets damaged by the wind. Scientists have developed rice plants with shorter stalks, giving a higher **yield**.

Feeding the people

Major foods in China include rice and pork. These are foods that can easily be produced in large quantities. With so many mouths to feed, the Chinese have had to find ways of producing as much food as possible from every available piece of land.

Where is the most crowded city?

Japan

The most populated city is Tokyo, the capital of Japan.

True or False?
There are almost as many people in Mexico City as in all of Australia.

Answers on page 31

In 2007, the city of Tokyo had nearly 13 million inhabitants. The whole of Greater Tokyo had more than 35 million inhabitants.

Downtown Tokyo

Which Places Have the Most Extreme Weather?

Some places have such extreme weather that no one is able to live there all the time, but people still go there to work. In some of these places, special clothes and buildings are needed to protect people from the weather.

Ethiopia

Dallol is an old volcanic crater in Ethiopia, Africa. The ground there is totally dry and lifeless. The air is extremely hot—the average temperature is 94.1° Fahrenheit (34.5° C). People cannot live there all year round, but some people make a living there by collecting natural salt that has collected on the ground.

Dallol

Where is the coldest place to work?

Life is tough at the weather research station of Eureka on Ellesmere Island in the Canadian territory of Nunavut. The temperature can be as low as –29° Fahrenheit (–34° C). When it is this cold, it is dangerous to go outside without special protective clothing. There is no sunlight there between mid-October and late February. Even in summer, the temperature is never more than 68° Fahrenheit (20° C).

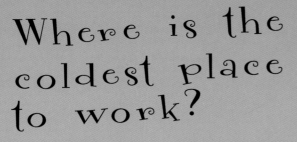

True or False?
People living in very high places have much larger lungs than other people.

?

?

Answers on page 31

Eureka

Ellesmere Island

Where Do People Live Longest?

In many parts of the world, people now tend to live longer than their parents or grandparents did. But the Japanese island of Okinawa has a greater percentage of people who live to be a hundred than anywhere else in the world.

Japan

Okinawa

Where do people not live very long?

In the world's poorest countries, people tend not to live as long as people in richer countries. Many people do not have enough food because of **famine** or war. Many do not have access to doctors, drugs, or hospitals when they need them.

Health education

In **developing countries** many lives are saved by teaching women how to ensure good **hygiene** and **nutrition** even under very difficult conditions.

Why do Okinawans live so long?

The people of Okinawa eat a healthy diet with little fat or salt, and they get plenty of exercise. People who reach the age of 97 hold a party to celebrate what they call their "return to childhood."

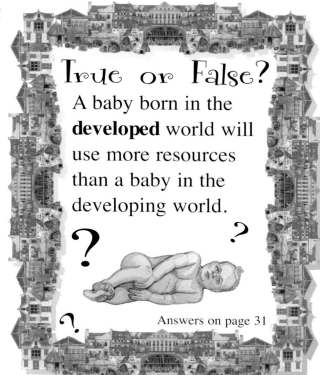

True or False?

A baby born in the **developed** world will use more resources than a baby in the developing world.

Answers on page 31

Why Are Some Places Dangerous to Live In?

There are many reasons why some places are more dangerous than others. Some place are more likely to experience natural disasters such as earthquakes, volcanic eruptions, **tsunamis**, hurricanes, floods, forest fires, avalanches, and droughts. There may also be human-made dangers such as warfare and violent crime.

True or False?

Most volcanoes lie along **faults** between parts of the earth's surface.

Answers on page 31

Volcano erupting

What's a tsunami?

A tsunami is a huge wave, usually caused by an earthquake under the sea. The energy from the earthquake sends vibrations through the water like huge ripples. The ripples travel very fast and hit with enormous force when they reach land. Most tsunamis occur in the Pacific Ocean.

Tsunamis can cause terrible floods that drown people, wipe out crops, and destroy or damage buildings. People who survive the flood are still in danger from starvation or disease.

Tsunami

When the wave reaches land, it may be up to 100 feet (30 m) high.

Flooding caused by a tsunami

Where Are the Oldest Buildings?

Egypt

The very first buildings that people made have disappeared. They were probably made of materials like mud, wood, and straw, which rot away over time. The buildings that survive longest are those that are made of stone.

Building in stone takes a lot of effort, so stone was not used for ordinary people's houses. It was used for grand buildings and monuments.

The Great Pyramid of Cheops at Giza in Egypt is one of the wonders of the ancient world. It was finished around 2560 B.C. When it was new, it was covered with a smooth layer of shiny white marble.

True or False?

Egypt is not the only country that has pyramids. **?**

Answers on page 31

Why was the Great Pyramid built?

The Great Pyramid was built as a tomb for the Egyptian **pharaoh** Cheops, or Khufu. The ancient Egyptians believed that as long as a dead person's body was preserved, their soul would survive.

A pyramid could take twenty or thirty years to build. The body of the dead king was laid to rest in a chamber at the center of the pyramid, surrounded by sacred texts carved into the stone walls.

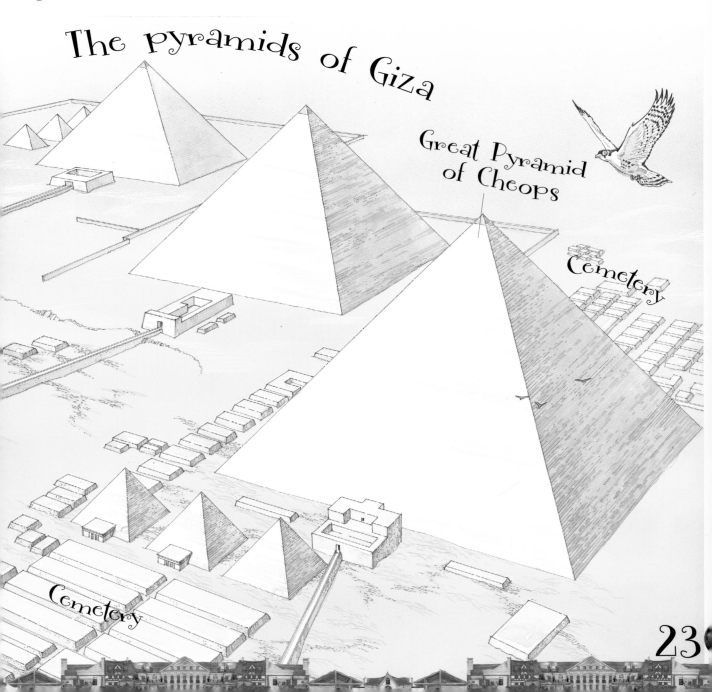

The pyramids of Giza

Great Pyramid of Cheops

Cemetery

Cemetery

How Tall Are the Tallest Structures?

Empire State Building: 1,250 feet (381 m)
New York City, 1931.
Currently the world's ninth tallest building—
it was the tallest for 41 years.

Burj Dubai: 2,000 feet (610 m) +
Dubai, United Arab Emirates (under construction). It will be the tallest building in the world when completed.

CN Tower: 1,815 feet (553 m)
Toronto, Canada, 1976.

Shanghai World Finance Centre: 1,614 feet (492 m)
Shanghai, China, 2007.

Sears Tower: 1,450 feet (442 m)
Chicago, 1974. Currently the tallest building in the United States.

Jin Mao Tower: 1,381 feet (421 m)
Shanghai, China, 1999.

ifc (International Finance Centre): 1,362 feet (415 m)
Hong Kong, China, 2003.

Freedom Tower: 1,776 feet (541 m)
New York City (under construction)

Taipei 101: 1,670 feet (509 m)
Taipei, Taiwan, 2004.
The world's tallest building in 2008.

Petronas Towers: 1,483 feet (452 m)
Kuala Lumpur, Malaysia, 1998.

Landmark Tower: 971 feet (296 m)
Yokohama, Japan, 1993.

Central Plaza: 1,227 feet (374 m) Hong Kong, China, 1992.

Burj Al Arab: 1,053 feet (321 m) Dubai, UAE, 2000.

Eiffel Tower: 984 feet (300 m) Paris, France, 1889.

Bank of China Tower: 1,209 feet (369 m) Hong Kong, China, 1990.

Canary Wharf Tower: 800 feet (244 m) London, England, 1990.

How Do People Harm the Places They Live In?

People cause harm to the places where they live and work in many different ways. They cut down trees for timber and they clear land for building on. They dig up the land to find coal and other **minerals**, and they drill into it for oil. They pollute land with garbage and the waste products of industry.

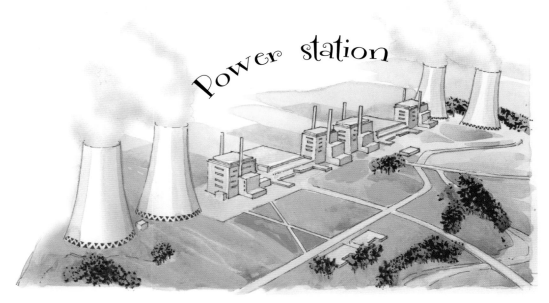

Power station

Most people think of electricity as a clean form of energy. But it has to be produced by power stations, and power stations cause pollution.

True or False?

People can get by without forests.

Answers on page 31

What is deforestation?

Deforestation means destroying forests by cutting down trees and not planting new ones. When the trees are destroyed, many of the animals that live in them die. The soil may wash away because there are no tree roots to hold it together.

27

What Other Places Have People Explored?

Modern technology allows people to survive in the most unlikely places. Humans have now visited the summits of the tallest mountains, the bottoms of the deepest oceans, the North and South Poles, and even the moon.

True or False?
The **bathyscaphe** submarine *Trieste* made the world's deepest dive in 1960.

Answers on page 31

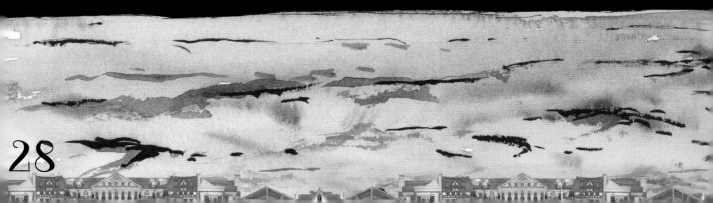

28

Central Plaza:
1,227 feet (374 m) Hong Kong, China, 1992.

Burj Al Arab: 1,053 feet (321 m) Dubai, UAE, 2000.

Eiffel Tower: 984 feet (300 m) Paris, France, 1889.

Bank of China Tower: 1,209 feet (369 m) Hong Kong, China, 1990.

Canary Wharf Tower: 800 feet (244 m) London, England, 1990.

How Do People Harm the Places They Live In?

People cause harm to the places where they live and work in many different ways. They cut down trees for timber and they clear land for building on. They dig up the land to find coal and other **minerals**, and they drill into it for oil. They pollute land with garbage and the waste products of industry.

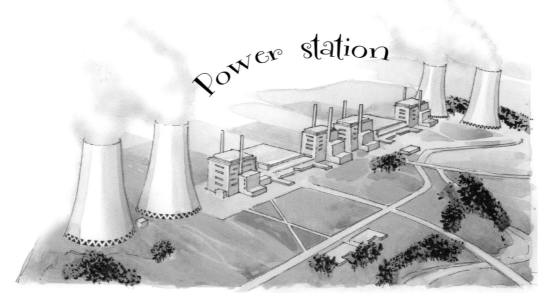

Power station

Most people think of electricity as a clean form of energy. But it has to be produced by power stations, and power stations cause pollution.

Answers on page 31

True or False?

People can get by without forests.

What is deforestation?

Deforestation means destroying forests by cutting down trees and not planting new ones. When the trees are destroyed, many of the animals that live in them die. The soil may wash away because there are no tree roots to hold it together.

27

What Other Places Have People Explored?

Modern technology allows people to survive in the most unlikely places. Humans have now visited the summits of the tallest mountains, the bottoms of the deepest oceans, the North and South Poles, and even the moon.

True or False?

The **bathyscaphe** submarine *Trieste* made the world's deepest dive in 1960.

Answers on page 31

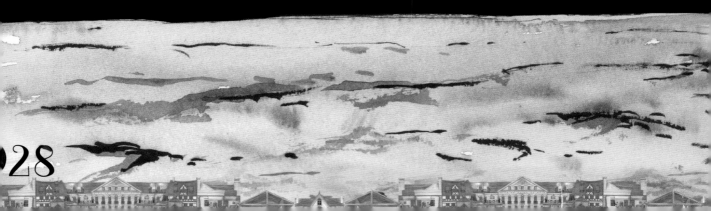

Where next?

One day, it may be possible to set up research bases on the moon for scientists to live and work in. It may be possible to grow food in special **biospheres** and to make oxygen for breathing.

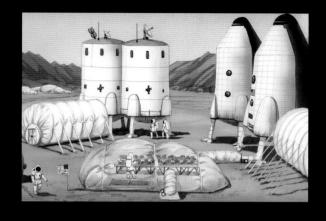

Who landed on the moon?

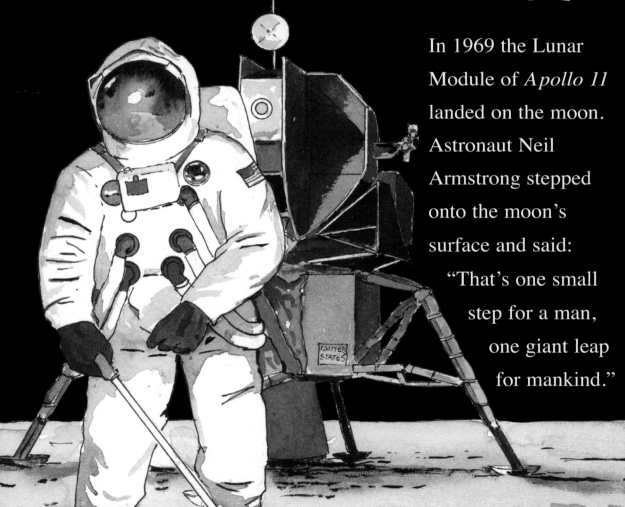

In 1969 the Lunar Module of *Apollo 11* landed on the moon. Astronaut Neil Armstrong stepped onto the moon's surface and said: "That's one small step for a man, one giant leap for mankind."

Useful Words

Bathyscaphe A deep-sea submarine.

Biosphere An airtight container in which plants can be grown.

Climate The weather that is typical of a particular area.

Deforestation The removal of forests or trees.

Developed country A country that has high levels of industry and many people living in cities.

Developing country A relatively poor country that has lower levels of industry and where most people live and work on the land.

Domestication The turning of wild animals and plants into farm animals and plants.

Famine A dangerous shortage of food.

Fault A place where two sections of the earth's surface meet.

Hunter-gatherers People who live by hunting animals and gathering wild plants to eat.

Hygiene The practice of keeping oneself clean and healthy.

Mineral Any useful substance that is found in the ground, such as oil, metals, or coal.

Nutrition Healthy eating.

Pharaoh A king of ancient Egypt.

Tsunami A massive wave, usually caused by an undersea earthquake.

Yield The amount of usable food that can be obtained from a crop.

Aztec pyramid

Answers

Page 7 FALSE! Fire has been used by people for at least half a million (500,000) years. Making fire is one of the most useful human inventions. It can be used for cooking, keeping warm, scaring away wild animals, making pottery and making metal objects.

Page 10 TRUE! It is easier to make houses out of wood, but mammoth bones were used in places where there was a shortage of wood.

Page 13 TRUE! The Sumerians made marks on clay tablets to keep records of the goods they bought and sold. At first the marks were pictures of the actual goods, but as time passed they changed from pictures to simplified signs.

Page 15 TRUE! Mexico City is home to about 20 million people, while Australia has about 21 million.

Page 17 FALSE! In high mountains such as the Andes and Himalayas, the air has less oxygen in it than it has lower down. The people who live there are able to breathe the thin air without any problems, but they do not have much larger lungs than other people. They do have more red cells in their blood, which helps them to use more oxygen from the air that they breathe.

Page 19 TRUE! People who live in developed countries use up far more of the Earth's resources than people in developing countries. They are more likely to drive cars, for example, and to own gadgets that use a lot of electricity.

Page 20 TRUE! Fault lines are cracks in the Earth's crust. Volcanoes occur when pressure beneath the crust forces molten (melted) rock to squirt out through a fault. Earthquakes occur on fault lines too.

Page 22 TRUE! The Aztec, the Maya, and other ancient peoples of South and Central America built temples to their gods in the shape of pyramids. These pyramids have stepped sides and a platform at the top where offerings were made. The pyramid-shaped temples of Mesopotamia are called ziggurats.

Page 27 FALSE! Forests are important for many reasons. Trees take in carbon dioxide and release oxygen—and humans need oxygen to breathe. Many useful foods and medicines come from plants or animals that live only in forests.

Page 28 TRUE! *Trieste* reached a depth of 6.8 miles (10.9 km) in the Mariana Trench, the deepest part of the Pacific Ocean.

Index

(Illustrations are shown in **bold type**.)